Mega-Tsunami

Mega-Tsunami

♦

The True Story of the Hebrew Exodus from Egypt

Robert S. Salzman

iUniverse, Inc.
New York Lincoln Shanghai

Mega-Tsunami
The True Story of the Hebrew Exodus from Egypt

Copyright © 2005 by Robert S. Salzman

All rights reserved. No part of this book may be used or reproduced by any means, graphic, electronic, or mechanical, including photocopying, recording, taping or by any information storage retrieval system without the written permission of the publisher except in the case of brief quotations embodied in critical articles and reviews.

iUniverse books may be ordered through booksellers or by contacting:

iUniverse
2021 Pine Lake Road, Suite 100
Lincoln, NE 68512
www.iuniverse.com
1-800-Authors (1-800-288-4677)

ISBN-13: 978-0-595-34797-1 (pbk)
ISBN-13: 978-0-595-67156-4 (cloth)
ISBN-13: 978-0-595-79531-4 (ebk)
ISBN-10: 0-595-34797-5 (pbk)
ISBN-10: 0-595-67156-X (cloth)
ISBN-10: 0-595-79531-5 (ebk)

Printed in the United States of America

"The Wind Blew, and the Water Piled High Like a Wall"[1]

---
1. Ancient Hebrew Text

Contents

Foreword xi

Chapter 1	The Adventure Begins 1
Chapter 2	Santorini Revisited 3
Chapter 3	Santorini Triggers the Quest 11
Chapter 4	The Ten Plagues 15
Chapter 5	The Time Line of Events 37
Chapter 6	A Trip to Sinai 47
Chapter 7	The Defining Moment 49
Chapter 8	The Nature of Miracles 51
Chapter 9	Hatshepsut Leads the Way 57
Chapter 10	A Papyrus Shop in Cairo 61
Chapter 11	Disaster 65
Chapter 12	The Ten Commandments 69
Chapter 13	A Divine Plan? 71
Chapter 14	Mega Tsunamis and Other Cataclysmic Events Yet to Come 75
Chapter 15	A Walk Along the Country Road 77
Chapter 16	Reprise 81

A Final Word From the Author 83
Index 85

ACKNOWLEDGEMENTS

I would like to thank my darling wife, Celia, who stood by me these many months, as I typed away at my desk. I know that I ignored her, drove her crazy with outbursts of enthusiasm, and bouts of lingering doubt.

I would also like to thank Professor Bob Brier of Long Island University and of the Discovery and Learning Channel fame, who was my mentor as I tried to make sense of all the conflicting data. Without his kindness, inspiration, and sound advice, this book would never have been written.

I would also like to thank David Korn of the NSIDC, in Boulder Colorado, who supplied me with the data for the Greenland ice-cores. Without this data, I could have never understood the significance of the biblical time lines.

I also would like to thank Jim Redzinak, an old friend, who illustrated the cover of this book.

I would like to thank the efficient librarians at the Wilbour Library, Brooklyn Museum of Art, who assisted me in finding many useful articles that greatly contributed to this book.

And lastly, I would like to thank a most charming and helpful librarian by the name of Robert Nelson of the Millington, NJ Library, who labored diligently to bring me the books I needed for my research.

Foreword

The recent tragedy in the Indian Ocean caused by the devastating tsunami events, has riveted the attention of the world. Despite all the interest, this was not the reason that I decided to write this book about a major tsunami. True, the title "Mega-Tsunami" is an attention grabber. However, it is the awesome power of the tsunami, which gives credence to the true story of the EXODUS, which will hereinafter unfold before you within these pages like lovely petals of a budding flower.

It is useful to present this story now, at a time when the greater awareness of the general public will properly guide their understanding and interpretation of the events that were wrought by the cataclysms some 3,000 years ago.

My world travels, and in particular my several visits to Santorini Island inspired this book. Santorini and its volcanic mountain is unique. The Santorini cataclysms, coupled with my scientific research at the Wilbour Library, and my research into the Greenland Ice-Cores, triggered my interest in linking Santorini's volcanic activity to the events of the Exodus.

Attempt is not made here to sensationalize the subject of the EXODUS. The events of history stand upon their own stage. This was a defining moment in time. The Exodus, and the Ten Commandments, as no other event, before or since, has shaped the future of western civilization.

Rather, the intention is to offer a plausible, scientific, and natural explanation of how the Hebrew nation escaped from Egypt some 3,000 years ago.

The subject of the Jewish EXODUS has been greatly misunderstood by religious scholars, scientists, Egyptologists, archaeologists, and historians from its very inception. Part of the problem, has been the lack of information describing the events. This was a dark period in history. There is little of record besides the biblical texts giving accurate witness to the events of the plagues that befell Egypt. Most authorities on the Exodus disagree as to who was pharaoh at that time, but most agree that the time of the Exodus was 1,446/7 B.C.

As I will reveal in this book, this established date may also be in doubt.

Nothing was recorded about the tsunamis that came to the Nile delta. People of those times did not understand tsunami events. Nothing was recorded of the terrible volcanic dusts that more than likely ravaged the land. The final **Mega-tsunami** that rescued the Hebrew nation at the Sea of Reeds was recorded in biblical text as a "Parting of the Sea".[1]

There were conflicting time lines and conflicting witnessing of events.

As aforementioned, there is much controversy about the identity of the pharaoh during the Exodus. Most of the books written by renowned archaeologists and Egyptologists, disagree about the pha-

---

1. The biblical text of the Exodus describes two walls of water, both to the left and right of the Hebrew nation. It will be suggested later within this book, that the unique terrain on the north shore of Egypt, next to the Sea of Reeds, actually divided the tsunami wall into two parts; a right and left wall of water.

raoh of the Exodus. And the richest source of information, the biblical texts are silent.

Cecile B. DeMille in the film, The Ten Commandments, suggested that Sethi and Rameses II were the pharaohs of the Exodus. He based his conclusion on work of historians of biblical times, such as Josephus and Philo. He claimed that even though they wrote in the era of Jesus, they nonetheless had access to ancient texts that were long ago destroyed or lost.

The problem with his assertion, however, is that Ramses II is recorded in the dynastic time line as having lived some two hundred years after the generally accepted time for the EXODUS of 1,446 B.C., i.e. Ramses II reign was recorded as from 1,224 to 1,290 B.C.

I suggest that this mystery can be resolved. My careful research into archives at the Wilbour Library of the Brooklyn Museum, and the Greenland Ice-Core data, suggests the time of the Exodus to have taken place somewhere between 1,264 and 1,288 B.C., during Ramses II reign.

The pharaoh, Ramses II, a great pharaoh king, was most probably the pharaoh of the Exodus, because the biblical text of the Exodus states that the Hebrew nation built the cities of Ramses and Pithom. Ramses city, named for the great pharaoh king, was lost for centuries. It has been recently excavated in the Nile delta near the city of Tallen. Six hundred stables were found for his 600 chariots.

I have also observed that few archaeologists and Egyptologists have made the absolute connection between the multiple eruptions on Santorini with the problems they created in the Nile delta of Egypt only 500 miles away.

The enormous eruptions immediately preceding the explosion, and the explosion itself, of Santorini, created events upon distant shores throughout the Mediterranean.

We know that such events have far-flung consequences, for we ourselves have recently witnessed the present tsunami events in the Indian Ocean. The tsunami in the Indian Ocean also carried towards Africa and Australia, many hundreds, if not thousands, of miles away.

As a final word, it is desired that the great scholars, rabbis, and scientists of today who may read this book, may find some time from their busy pursuits to add their knowledge and thoughts to the story that I have told here. It would be helpful if the glass found in the Greenland Ice-Cores for the periods of 1,440 to 1,450 B.C., and/or for 1,289 to 1,265 B.C., would be examined and determined whether it came from Santorini Island.

Most of all, I hope that the general public will find this humble work entertaining and informative.

1

The Adventure Begins

I looked out upon the beautiful Aegean Sea from the summit of Santorini Island. The mountainside of Santorini was a panorama of whitewashed homes, shops, tavernas, and villas. Our cruise ship, the Stella Solaris, had departed on the previous day from the Greek port of Piraeus. We had sailed south to Crete, and had visited the temples of King Minos. Then we sailed eastward, and headed toward this wonderful, magical land, Santorini Island. The early afternoon was filled with the happy and busy sounds of the Greek tavernas, the shops, and the donkey owners, who guided their friendly companions up and down the mountain at a brisk pace.

The sea had a compelling tranquility as evening approached. The sky was golden with sun, and the maroon color of the Aegean was not unlike the wine that flowed so freely in the restaurants nearby. The evening breeze graced my cheek, and I stood transfixed at the beauty of this place.

At this time, I knew nothing about the tragedy that had befallen this island some 3,000 years ago. I am not sure whether I wanted to know. My thoughts were focused upon my lovely blond wife, whose sculptured looks silently emulated the Greek goddesses of old.

I was a young man, who had not read much about the ancient world. Yes, I had read Homer's Iliad and Odyssey. But, my experiences were very limited. I had become interested in inventions, and my thoughts rarely deviated from science.

Perhaps, if time would permit, it might be possible to see the world, and learn of other societies and cultures.

It never occurred to me, that I would be returning to this beautiful place several times, and each time I would take home another clue about the truth of the EXODUS.

2

Santorini Revisited

Twenty years had passed since my first visit to Greece, and I found myself once more in this ancient land. In a few days, I was to sail with my new bride for the Greek Isles, and Santorini was on the itinerary.

Now, I held a different beautiful woman under my arm. She was, and still is, a buxom, green-eyed beauty. She was, and still is, a wonderful traveling companion. Perchance, I would be able to see once more, that lovely island, "Santorini", whose memory I had carefully tucked away within the recesses of my mind. Would it not be a treat to cuddle with my new sweetheart by the sea at sunset?

◆ ◆ ◆

Athens, so vibrant and exciting rose up before me. The weather almost always perfect in the land of the Greeks put me in a marvelous mood. With such nice weather, I hated to go indoors to visit the museum of Archaeology. But, someone had informed me, that a Greek archaeologist by the name of Spirodin Marinatos had just unearthed the lost city of Akrotiri on the Island of Thera (The old name for Santorini Island). The lovely frescos of the ancient Minoan people were being exhibited in the museum in Athens in a special section dedicated to the discovery. Certainly, this was no time to worry about getting a tan.

As my new wife and I made our way up the long flights of stairs, I came to a roped-off section marked: "special exhibit". Surely, this must be the exhibit they had been talking about.

As I approached the attendant at the desk in front of the maroon-roped barrier, he said that the fee for entrance was Ten Dollars. I opened my wallet in order to withdraw a freshly minted twenty-dollar bill. Carefully, I placed the bill in the attendant's hand, and after receiving two tickets, my wife and I briskly moved forward in anticipation. To my thorough delight, the walls of the museum were covered with the Minoans in joyful play and work-a-day pursuits. There was a young Minoan fisherman carrying a number of fish in each hand. There were maidens gamboling gleefully towards me through centuries of antiquity. They carried spiraling threads of red and gold in each hand as they ran. My fertile imagination was in full bloom, and in my mind, I ran along side them as they unfurled those rapturous threads before me.

But, even as I thought about the art, I kept asking myself, who was this Greek archaeologist named Spirodin Marinatos, and how did he come to find such unusual treasures? What had covered these lovely works of art for over thirty-five hundred years?

Back in my hotel room, I poured over the brochures that they had given me at the museum. I read the history of Akrotiri.

Akrotiri was a Minoan city built around the Thera (Santorini) volcano that was to doom its existence.

Spirodin Marinatos had found pumice on Crete, and realized that it had to have come from the Santorini volcano, only seventy-five miles away. He had talked with the farmers, who had tilled the rich volcanic soil along the cliffs of Santorini. They had found several artifacts of ancient origin. Many had told of people being swallowed, or disappearing into the soil. Spirodin had suspected that the city of Akrotiri lay below. Several workmen and farmers started digging under his direction, and about fifteen feet down they hit the top of a dwelling. After many months of excavating, a few streets were laid bare for the eyes to behold. Beautiful buildings with winding staircases were unearthed. There was homes with indoor plumbing on the upper floors. This was quite remarkable, for a civilization that thrived thirty-five hundred years ago. This was a magnificent civilization that suddenly came to an end.

Only a small portion of the city had been excavated during my last visit. Spirodin was accidentally killed, when he fell off a wall in Akrotiri. This temporarily halted the excavation, but the work he started continues today. Only the lack of funds prevents a greater unearthing of this city.

Spirodin suspected that a terrible eruption had taken place on the volcanic island, and had covered the city in pumice and ash. The volcanic eruption effectively brought an end to the Minoan city. This eruption was followed a generation later (as then reported) by one of the largest explosions of modern times. A huge tsunami was created by the blast, which rushed at two hundred miles per hour towards Crete and the Minoan fleet, thus bringing an end to the thriving Minoan economy. The hot magma that spewed from the magma chamber burned the palaces of King Minos only 75 miles away.

Today, one can see a line along the earthen cliffs sloping up from the sea at Crete's port of Iraklion. This line, which faces towards Santorini, was the top of the Tsunami that had hit Crete, and laid waste to the Minoan fleet of ten thousand ships. This line two hundred feet above the village is an indication of the occurrence of a MEGA-TSUNAMI.

That this took place is not in doubt, because similar eruptions and earthquakes of the still active volcano of Santorini, periodically produce tsunamis at Iraklion. The local fishermen often stand dumbstruck, as the sea rushes out, leaving little sea creatures and fish to flap helplessly in the denuded seabed. Then, almost by magic they witness a wall of water rushing towards shore.

But there was more to the mystery that destroyed the Minoan fleet, and the Golden Trade Triangle between the three cities of Iraklion, Alexandria, and Ephesis. Spirodin in all his diggings did not find one body in Akrotiri. This gave rise to the speculation that an earlier eruption had caused the Minoans to flee, and never return.

◆ ◆ ◆

The tragedy of the volcanic eruption that doomed Pompei and Herculaneum in central Italy, had yielded several bodies, and it was most unusual that nothing of human remains could be found in Akrotiri.

At Pompei, the bodies were recreated by plaster filling the vacant crevices within the earth. This revealed the human shapes of several unfortunate people, who had been incinerated, in their last desperate struggle for life. The fifth pyroclastic flow from Vesuvius had finally reached the city limits of Pompei, thus incinerating and choking all the life forms in the city.

At Herculaneum, skeletal bodies were found in underground vaults. Their flesh had been instantly incinerated by a 400 degree pyroclastic flow that came down the mountain at 200 miles an hour.

◆ ◆ ◆

Most of the Island of Thera (the old name for Santorini) had exploded, when seawater rushed into the magma chamber through vents in the sea wall. The vents were created by earlier eruptions, which were of great magnitude in their own right, as I have observed from Greenland ice-core data.

The blast that took place caused an explosion that is estimated to have displaced 30 to 40 cubic kilometers of hot magma. The whole magma chamber was blasted into the air. The cataclysm was so immense, that most of the island was obliterated, leaving a huge caldera reaching to a depth of one third of a mile. To put the blast in perspective, this cataclysm would have made most other volcanic events of recent and biblical times, look like dwarfs. It has been estimated that the explosion was 3.5 times as great as that of Krakatoa Island, which killed an estimated 40,000 people in Sumatra during the late eighteen hundreds.[1]

To summarize, what the scientists had finally concluded through the study of the ash deposits, and other identifying evidence, was the existence of a prior eruption of great magnitude in its own right, just prior to the great explosion, which forced the Akrotirians from their island. The Akrotirians sailed from their island never to return. They left their homes, and the streets of their city bare and lifeless.

Just prior to the main explosive event, the volcano on Thera had launched what I have interpreted from Greenland ice-core data, several major eruptions. One of the major eruptions blew a cloud of ash and pumice high into the stratosphere. I believe that this ash was carried with prevailing southeasterly winds towards Egypt.

I believe that this eruption created a cloud of ash that drifted towards the Nile delta. The cloud eventually obscured the sun over the Nile delta cities of Ramses and Pithom. The cloud turned day into night for three days.

---

1. Some estimates have calculated the explosion as much as 10 to 14 times that of Krakatoa.

The eruption also produced a more immediate result. A tsunami was created, that rolled into the Nile delta. The wave of seawater caused the fresh waters of the Nile tributaries to become brackish. The brackish water produced a red tide, that the ancient populace thought was blood.

◆ ◆ ◆

Now, as I sailed upon a cruise ship, I found myself once more approaching that white-capped jewel, called Santorini Island. The island comprises a barren shell of the old volcanic mountain. A donkey ride can take you up and down from the sea to the city of white that graces its pinnacles.

In recent times, a tram has been built, which quickly delivers you to your destination. I prefer the donkeys, the ride is slower, but you do not want to be rushed about, when you are in Greece. The path is narrow and winding, and occasionally, a donkey may bump against the stone walled edge. Not to fear, they are pretty sure-footed. Just be sure to ride a donkey who has not been thoroughly overworked.[2]

---

2. The operators of the donkey train, press the animals pretty hard, so that they can service as many people as possible. The competition with the tram has only exacerbated the hectic conditions that already existed.

3

Santorini Triggers the Quest

Santorini island, oh so beautiful, are thee not most fair and exotic? How wistfully I could dream forever folded in your embrace.

It was here, on my third trip to Santorini Island, ten years later, that my thoughts of a tsunami event being responsible for the EXODUS began to control my thoughts. Could Santorini's cataclysm be responsible for the so-called "parting of the Sea of Reeds"? Slowly, the thought began to invade the upper regions of my waking conscious state. It was no great epiphany, but a slow gradual awakening.

Five hundred miles to the southeast of Santorini Island stands the Nile Delta, and no intervening barrier lies in between, except for one or two small islands.

There, in the Nile delta, upon silt and fine sand of the delta mud, a great wave came roaring forward. There upon the silt and sand were built the twin cities of Ramses and Pithom. The cities of Ram-Pi, next to the Hebrew town of Goshen, near the Sea of Reeds. Here it was that the Hebrew slaves had toiled so arduously to build the temples and monuments of pharaoh. Here it was that pharaoh had cast them out, because of all the plagues that had descended upon the Egyptian populace. But then, pharaoh had changed his mind, and sought after them to perhaps restore his honor amongst his people, who had begun to question his power to rule, or as revenge. Thus, the final act was cast in stone.

The water had been sucked out in advance of the great wall of water of the Mega-tsunami reaching Egypt's north shore. This allowed the Hebrew nation to walk through the denuded seabed of the Sea of Reeds, and onto higher ground. The pursuing Egyptians were just too late. The pride of the Egyptian charioteers were caught by the advancing wall of water, and cast into the sea. The water had previously receded, just as it had done at the shores at Iraklion. The terrifying wall of water came to greet the 600 charioteers.

4

The Ten Plagues

I have already hinted as to what caused some of the Ten Plagues in the previous chapter. Before I even came upon the article by Jeffrey A. Lee, "Explaining the Plagues of Egypt", The Skeptical Inquirer, Nov./Dec. 2004; 28, 6, Research Library, Pages 52 through 54., I had already formed some ideas about the Ten Plagues being the result of natural events. The difference with my theories, however, is that I link the driving force of these natural events to the cataclysms of the Thera volcano.

♦ ♦ ♦

Several years later after my Santorini visits, I found myself attending morning services at the Jewish Community Center of Summit, New Jersey.

Every Monday, I would attend the synagogue to participate in Minion services. Always, I read the same text: "The mighty lord saved Israel, and the flower of Egypt's charioteers were sent hurtling into the sea."

"The wind blew, and the water piled high like a wall".

This very descriptive ancient text was so intriguing, that I thought that it surely must be describing a tsunami. Was this merely poetry, or was it truly descriptive of what had happened those many years ago?

It was hard to formulate that the "Parting of the Sea" was caused by a tsunami. Old ideas die hard, and even when one faces the truth, it is difficult to divorce oneself from the ingrained prior teachings. Did the seas really part, or was it a tsunami?

There were more bits and pieces that began to connect. In the first instance, we had learned that there were large eruptions before the island of Santorini exploded. The volcanic eruptions hurled ash and pumice high into the stratosphere, and it is most probable that the ash traveled sufficiently south to have obscured the sun over the cities of Ramses and Pithom for three days.

Severe and unusual weather effects, such as: "Hail", weather inversions, and lightning bolts, etc., often accompany large volcanic eruptions.

We know that such major eruptions can obscure the sun many miles away. One just has to remember the explosion of Mount St. Helens about twenty years ago. Fine pumice dust was distributed over 500 miles away with the prevailing winds. The sun was blocked out in many areas, and people who were driving during the day had to turn on their headlights. Day had literally turned to night in the western United States.

And as I recall, this lasted several days until prevailing winds blew the dust clouds away. Also, in many areas the settling dusts coated the countryside, and a lively trade developed, as some enterprising individuals started selling the pumice in jars as souvenirs.

◆　　◆　　◆

The Santorini eruptions were large enough to create tsunamis that rolled toward the Nile delta disrupting natural conditions in the tributaries. The first tsunami would have traveled into the low-lying Nile delta causing seawater to mix with the fresh waters of the Nile tributaries. When this happens, the water becomes brackish, and it is not uncommon for algae blooms to form, such as a "Red Tide". This would have looked like the sea had turned to blood.

And this phenomenon would be accompanied with the dying of fish, because they would be deprived of oxygen.

The darkness of the eruption brought by the dust would have disturbed the sleep cycles of small creatures in the kingdom. Locusts, and all manner of insects and small creatures may have started to swarm, thus giving rise to the other plagues that were recorded.

And would not have this pestilence given rise to the further contamination of the water, to further compound the contamination wrought by the glass filled dusts that must have descended upon the Egyptian populace.

Cattle in the fields would have started to die from eating and ingesting the glass-filled dusts that covered the grasses and that covered the land.

Now it is written in the biblical text, that Goshen was spared all of these calamities. I would venture to suggest that the falling dusts did not evenly distribute themselves. I suggest that the cities of Ramses and Pithom to the west of Goshen, bore the main brunt of the dust fallout. It would have all depended upon the prevailing winds, and the terrain.

I suggest, that the winds bearing the volcanic dusts of Thera, had circumvented the western flanks of Goshen, and landed in the cities of Ramses and Pithom to the west.

One might even suggest, that the taking of the first-born was disease related. How such a rapidly occurring plague, or disease could differentiate between Hebrew and Egyptian, and between first born and second born, is discussed later on.

It is important to follow the biblical text when trying to make the pieces fit.

It is my opinion that if the biblical text is in conflict with other evidence, one should rely on the biblical text. And I believe that the scientific evidence will prove the bible right.

As I admonish to all, before one can make the scientific pieces fit, one must look at the biblical text. We need to follow the time line of the bible. <u>The biblical text is almost always right.</u>

Therefore, let us begin. Let us explore how the Ten Plagues are reported.

◆ ◆ ◆

Chapter 5, Exodus: And the Lord, God of the Hebrews sent Moses and Aaron to speak to pharaoh. "Thus says the Lord, the God of Israel, "Let my people go, that they may hold a feast to me in the wilderness."" The same day pharaoh commanded the taskmasters, "You shall no longer give the people straw to make bricks, let them go and gather straw for themselves. Your work shall by no means be lessened in the least."

The Hebrew nation complained to Moses that he had made their plight worse.

And Moses said unto God, "Why didst thou ever send me? For since I came to pharaoh to speak in thy name, he has done evil to this people, and thou has not delivered thy people at all."

Chapter 6, Exodus: "But the Lord said to Moses, "Now you shall see what I will do to Pharaoh; for with a strong hand he will send them out, yea, with a strong hand he will drive them out of his land"".

Chapter 7, Exodus: God spoke to Moses, and commanded him to say to pharaoh in the morning as he is going out to water, and tell him to "Let my people go". Moses was commanded to strike the water in the Nile with his rod. The water turned to blood, and the fish died.

To me this is strongly suggestive of a red tide, or algae bloom. The strong, first eruption at Thera would have produced a large tsunami that roiled the waters in the tributaries of the Nile. Seawater would have mixed with the fresh water of the Nile delta tributaries, causing the water to turn brackish. This is an ideal condition for the forming of a Red Tide. Naturally the fish would have died from lack of oxygen. The river would have had an awful odor from all the rotting fish, and the ancient people would have associated the red color with blood. I am not the only researcher who has suggested this, and if it occurred to some one else, then it is not beyond logical reasoning to conclude this happened.

And as the biblical text reports:

"The Nile became foul, and the Egyptians were loathe to drink from it."

Seven days had passed after the Lord had struck the Nile.

Chapter 8, Then God commanded Moses to tell pharaoh that if he did not let the people go, he would plague all the country with frogs. And pharaoh told Moses if God would cause the frogs to leave, he would let the people go.

The frogs would have left the waters of the Nile, because of the lack of oxygen from the algae bloom.

And pharaoh was not true to his word, so the Lord commanded Aaron to strike the dust with the rod, and the land was afoul with gnats. Pharaoh still would not relent.

And then, God sent swarms of flies about the land, but he separated Goshen from the plague, so the Hebrew nation would not suffer this plague. Pharaoh then entreated Moses to go into the wilderness and ask God to remove the flies. And Moses asked God to remove the flies, and God complied. But pharaoh still did not relent.

The dying fish would have attracted gnats and flies.

Chapter 9, Exodus: And God commanded Moses to tell pharaoh that he would cause all the cattle in the field to die; horses, the asses, the camels, the herds, and the flocks. And again, the Lord made a distinction between the Egyptians and the Hebrew nation. None of the cattle of the Hebrews died.

Falling glass-filled dust traveling southeast from the eruption would have poisoned the grasses upon which the cattle fed, thus causing them to die. The prevailing wind circumvented Goshen.

And God commanded Moses to take ashes from the kiln, and in the sight of pharaoh, throw the ashes towards the sky. And the ashes became fine dust, and the dust afflicted all the Egyptians with boils. The boils broke out as sores on both man and beast. But still, the pharaoh would not let the Hebrew nation go.

The pestilence, unclean water, acid rain, and the glass-filled dusts may have been the cause of the Egyptian's boils.

Then, the Lord said: Behold, tomorrow at this time, I shall cause very heavy hail to fall. And those Egyptians who feared the Lord, gathered their cattle from the fields, so they would not perish from the hail. And God said unto Moses: "Stretch forth your hand toward heaven, that there may be hail in all the land of Egypt." And God sent thunder, hail, and flashing fire. The hail shattered trees and plants, but only in Goshen, was there no hail. And pharaoh entreated Moses to stop the hail, for he would let the people go. And Moses complied. But again pharaoh changed his mind.

The continuing eruptions on Thera would have caused bizarre weather effects creating weather inversions, hail, strong lightning, and thunder. The falling dust particles carry with it a charge, which creates a static electrical potential between the earth and the clouds. Lightning results, and the air masses become roiled with activity. Inversions of cold and warm air create the conditions for hail.

Chapter 10. Then, the Lord said to Moses, "Stretch out your hand over the land of Egypt for the locusts, that they may come upon the land of Egypt, and eat every plant in the land, all that the hail has left." And the locusts ate everything, but still the pharaoh would not let the people go.

It is not clear to scientists just how locusts swarm. Some scientists suggest it's a periodic cycle, and others suggest that it could be an event that requires some external cause to trigger it. Certainly a hailstorm could be one such event.

And the servants of pharaoh said: "How long shall this man (Moses) be a snare to us? Let the men go that they may serve the Lord their God; do you not yet understand that Egypt is ruined?"

But pharaoh refused to let the Hebrew nation go.

Then the Lord commanded Moses to stretch out his hand toward heaven, and there was darkness for three days. But all the people of Israel had light where they dwelt.

The eruptions on Thera gathering momentum, would produce enough dust and emissions to block out the sun for three days. The prevailing southeasterly wind would have blown towards the

Nile delta obscuring the sun over Ramses and Pithom. We have spoken of the migration of the dusts of Mount St. Helens, which obscured visibility hundreds of miles away. One must also observe, that the eruptions on Thera were of a much greater magnitude than those we witnessed at Mount St. Helens. It would not be unreasonable to state that a large portion of the Mediterranean would have been effected. Other archaeologists have made statements to the effect that the entire Mediterranean area surrounding Thera would have been severely harmed by the cataclysms.

Then the pharaoh said to Moses: "Get away from me; take heed to yourself; never see my face again; for in the day you see my face you shall die." And Moses said: "As you say! I will not see your face again."

Chapter 11, Exodus: The Lord said to Moses, "Yet one plague more I will bring upon Pharaoh and upon Egypt; afterwards he will let you go hence; when he lets you go, he will drive you away completely. Speak now in the hearing of the people, that they ask, every man of his neighbor, jewelry of silver and of gold." And the Lord gave the people favor in the eyes of the Egyptians. And Moses was very great in the land of Egypt, and in the sight of Pharaoh's servants and in the sight of the people.

And Moses said, "Thus says the Lord: About midnight I will go forth in the midst of Egypt; and all the first-born in the land of Egypt shall die, from the first-born of Pharaoh who sits upon his throne, even to the first-born of the maidservant who is behind the mill; and all the first born of the cattle. And there shall be a great cry throughout all the land of Egypt, such as there has never been, nor ever shall be again. But against any of the people of Israel, either man or beast, not a dog shall growl; that you may know that the lord makes a distinction between the Egyptians and Israel. And all these servants shall come down to me, saying, 'Get you out, and all the people who follow you.' And after that I will go out."

Chapter 12, Exodus: And the Lord said, "For I shall pass through the land of Egypt this night, and I will smite all the first-born in the land of Egypt, both man and beast, and on all the gods of Egypt I will execute judgments: I am the Lord."

And the Lord was true to his word, and there was a great cry in Egypt. And pharaoh sent for Moses and Aaron, and told them to leave Egypt.

Jeffrey Lee offers the explanation that dwindling food shortages caused the Egyptians to consume contaminated grain, thus causing a typhus plague. This would have favored the killing of the first-born. However, consider this: Goshen was located to the east of the main population centers of Ram-Pi. The sudden epidemic may have spared the Hebrews by reason of their remoteness to the main epidemic centers of Ramses and Pithom.

But also consider this: The Hebrew people isolated themselves in their homes during the night of the taking of the first-born. This would have been just as effective as a modern medical quarantine.

The lamb's blood they spread about their lentils and doorposts might have acted as a sealant around the entrances. The sticky lamb's blood could have acted to catch any stray dusts and particles, thus protecting the dwellers from a miasmic plague.

And was it Egyptian grain that was contaminated? Could the contamination have been in the yeast, of which the Hebrews did not partake when they baked matzoh, the bread without leavening?

Chapter 13, Exodus: And Moses said to the people, "Remember this day, in which you came out from Egypt, out of the house of bondage, for by strength of hand the Lord brought you out from this place; no leavened bread shall be eaten."

Consider this: God spared Goshen. And would the winds and their accompanying dusts have determined where the plagues were spread. How many times can you stand and watch a storm pouring rain to the earth only a mile away?

As a child, I remember standing across the street, and watching rainfall on the other side of the street, while I remained dry on the other side.

It is to be observed, that the Hebrews who practiced Kosher slaughter and preparation of cattle, may have protected themselves from the diseases in the meat that the Egyptians may have consumed.

◆   ◆   ◆

Thus, with dwindling food supplies and disease rampant everywhere, pharaoh may have also cast the Hebrew nation out of Egypt for economic reasons. Perhaps he considered them no longer an asset? These slaves may have now represented many mouths to feed in a time of famine. Perhaps pharaoh truly viewed the Hebrew God as the cause of his troubles? It is not certain his reasons, but cast the Hebrews out he did.

However, having cast them out, his troubles may have been compounded. The Egyptian people may now have considered him weak. Perhaps they viewed him as a lesser god, than the Hebrew god?

So it is with this turn of events, pharaoh changed his mind. He decided to pursue the Hebrew nation in order to show his people that he was still strong, or as a measure of his revenge.

Chapter 14, Exodus: And the Lord said to Moses: "Tell the people of Israel to turn back and encamp in front of Pi-ha-Hi'roth, between Migdol and the sea, in front of Ba'al-ze'phon; you shall encamp over against it, by the sea. For Pharaoh will say of the people of Israel, 'They are entangled in the land; the wilderness has shut them in.' And I will harden Pharaoh's heart, and he will pursue them and I will get glory over Pharaoh and all his host; and the Egyptians shall know that I am the Lord."

When the king of Egypt was told that the people had fled, the mind of Pharaoh and his servants was changed toward the people, and they said, "What is this we have done, that we have let Israel go from serving us?" So pharaoh made ready his chariot, and took six hundred picked chariots and all other chariots of Egypt with officers over all of them. And the Lord hardened the heart of Pharaoh King of Egypt and he pursued the people of Israel as they went forth defiantly. The Egyptians pursued them, all Pharaoh's horses and chariots and his horsemen and his army, and overtook them encamped at the sea, by pi-ha-hi'roth, in front of Ba'al-ze'phon.

When Pharaoh drew near, the people of Israel lifted up their eyes, and behold, the Egyptians were marching after them; and they were in great fear.

And Moses said to the people, "Fear not, stand firm, and the salvation of the Lord, which he will work for you today; for the Egyptians whom you see today, you shall never see again.

And the Lord said to Moses: "…tell the people of Israel to go forward. Lift up your rod, and stretch out your hand over the sea and divide it, so that the people of Israel may go on dry ground through the sea.

The tsunami comprising a two hundred high wall of water was advancing on the northern shore of Egypt. The water was being being sucked out of the Sea of Reeds ahead of the tsunami, thus leaving a dry seabed.

And the people of Israel went into the midst of the sea on dry ground, the waters being a wall to them on their right hand and on their left.[1] The Egyptians pursued, and went in after them into the midst of the sea, all Pharaoh's horses, his chariots, and his horsemen.

A wall of water advancing upon this place would have been split in half, and would have rushed on to shore in two parts. This would have presented to all observers a wall of water to both the right and left of them. [2]

---

1. *Owing to the unique terrain that presents itself at Ba'al-ze'phon, it appears that a tsunami rushing towards this area would have presented a wall rushing to both the left and right of the people. One will observe that the topography of Ba'al-ze'phon presents a triangular vertex toward the sea. The waters would have naturally divided about the outstanding promenance.*
2. I have seen only one other place where the sea rolls into shore from two separate angles, i.e. both to the left and right of the observer. Should one want to see one of the most unique and beautiful beaches in the world, take a trip to the middle island of Kaikos, in the Caribbean Sea. The beach that I talk about has rocks in the center over which the water cascades like a waterfall, and the sea rolls into shore from both the left and the right.

And in the morning watch the Lord in the pillar of fire and of cloud looked down upon the host of the Egyptians, and discomfited the host of the Egyptians,...

I suggest that the hot magma from the explosion on Santorini following the eruptions may have fallen to earth on the northern shores of Egypt in front of the Egyptians, as flaming sheets. This I suggest was the "Pillar of fire". Nearly 30 to 40 cubic Kilometers of hot magma were ejected from the magma chamber. The hot magma would have traveled at supersonic speed in a trajectory 500 miles towards Egypt. The Mega-Tsunami would have arrived later by reason of its slower speed of 200 miles per hour, i.e. the wave would have taken approximately two and one half hours to reach the north shore, whereas the magma would have reached Egypt in less than an hour.

Then the Lord said to Moses, "stretch out your hand over the sea, that the water may come back upon the Egyptians, upon their chariots, and upon their horsemen."...

◆ ◆ ◆

The biblical text speaks of "Yam Suph" as the place where the Hebrew nation crossed. "Yam Suph" translates as: "The Sea of Reeds". The Greeks mistakenly translated "Yam Suph" as the "Red Sea". Make no mistake, it was the Sea of Reeds, because the marshy terrain of Northern Egypt is just west of the town of Goshen. And it is this type of terrain at Ba'al-ze'phon that best fits the biblical text in the "parting of the sea" phenomena. The Encyclopedia Judaica (see map) shows the suggested route across the Sea of Reeds from Goshen, wherein the Hebrew nation encamped at Ba'al-Ze'phon by the sea. This terrain presents a unique triangular vertex towards the sea.

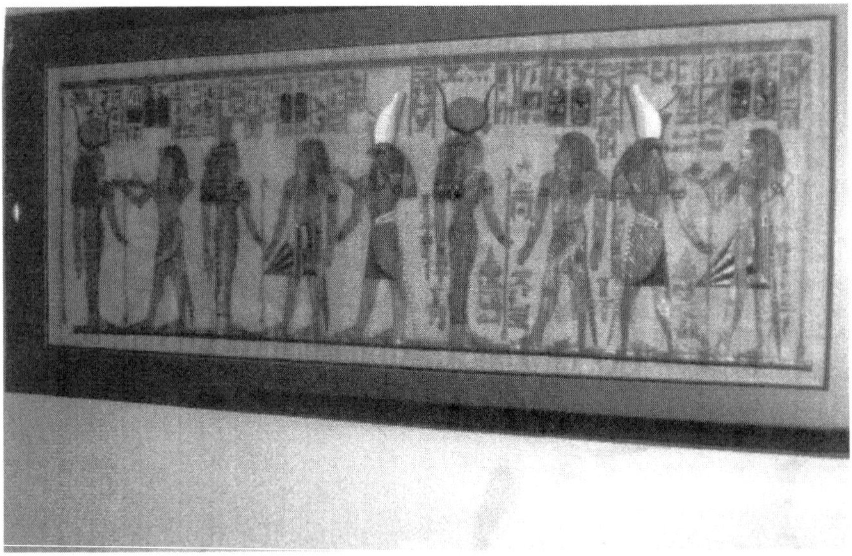

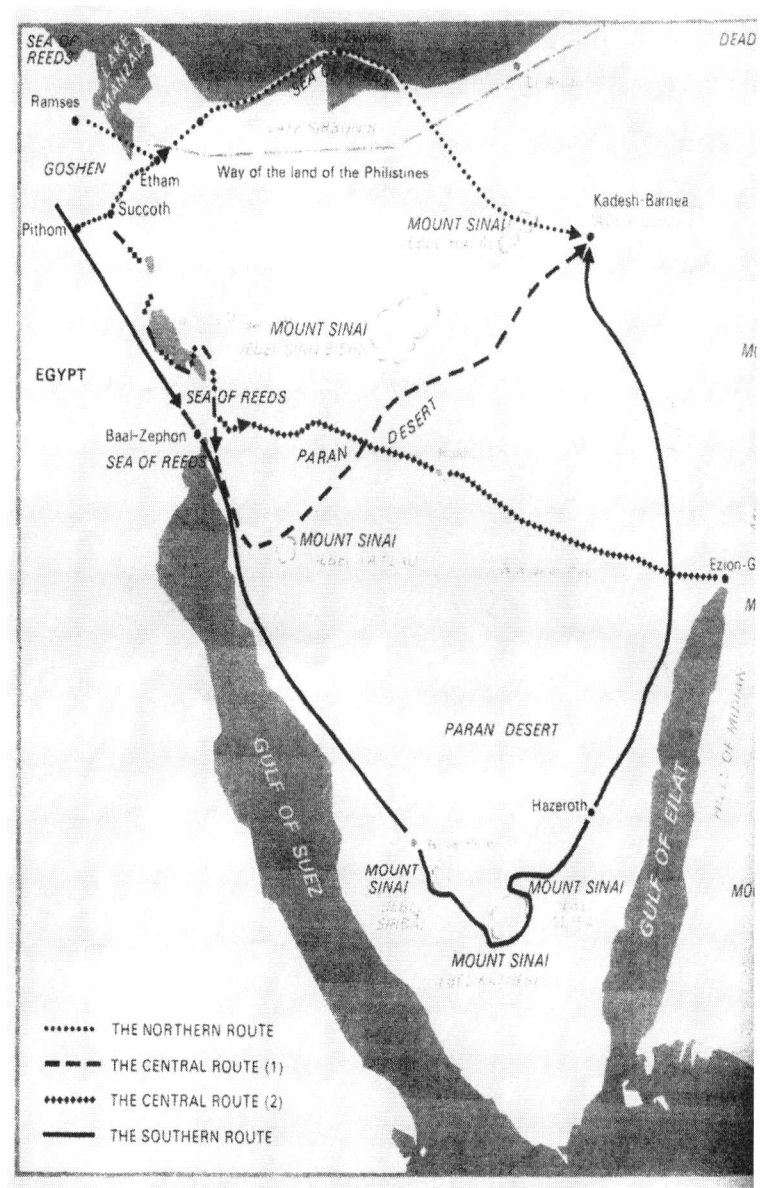

Map 1. Map illustrating major theories on the Israelites' route from Egypt to Kadesh-Barnea; in addition to the routes are given according to various theories.

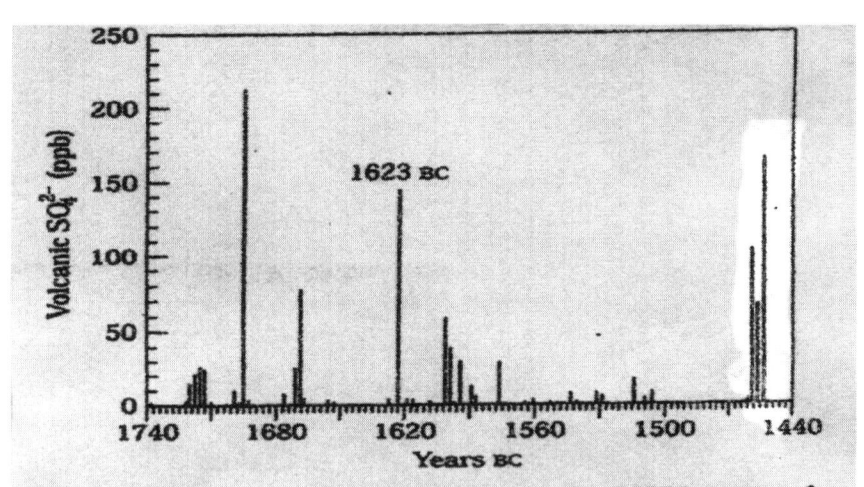

Figure 1. Volcanic SO_4^{2-} time series from the GISP2 ice core for the period between 1440 and 1740 BC. The signal at 1623 BC is highlighted.

SEA OF CRETE
MEDITERRANEAN S
DODECANESE
CYPRUS
Nicosia
Antalya
Isparta
Denizli
Aydin
Konya
Muğla
Elmali
Manavgat
Alanya (Coracesium)
Rodos
KARPATHOS
Iraklio (Candia)
KRITI
LIBYA
Libyan Plateau
(Ad Diffah)
Matrûh
EL ISKANDARIYA
(ALEXANDRIA)
Rashîd
Damanhûr
El Mahalla el Kubra
El Mansûra
Tanta
Zagazig
Bûr Sa'îd (Port Said)
Ismâ'ilîya
Shibîn el Kôm
EL GIZA
EL QAHIRA (CAIRO)
Helwân
El Suweis
El Faiyûm
Beni Suef
El Fashn
Maghâgha
Beni Mazâr
Samâlût
El Minya
Munkhafad el Qattâra
(Qattara Depression)
Qattâra
El Wâhât el Sîwa
El Wâhât El Bahariya
El Dab'a

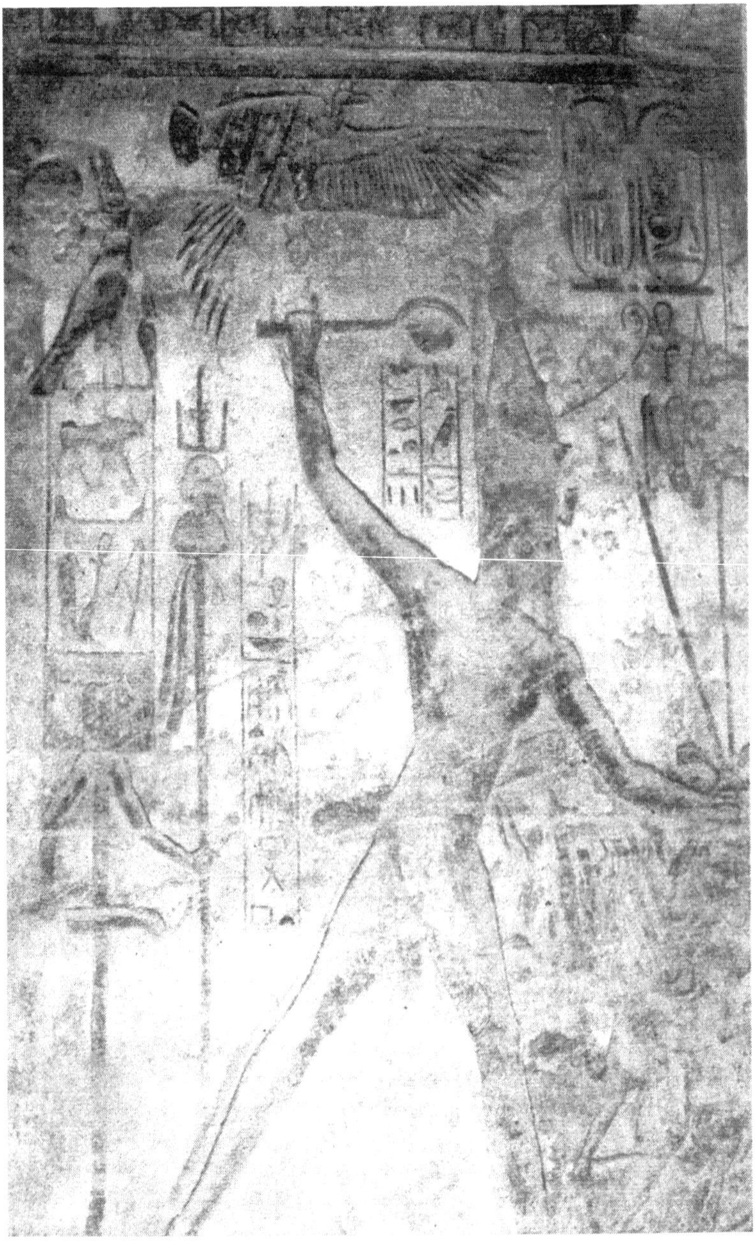

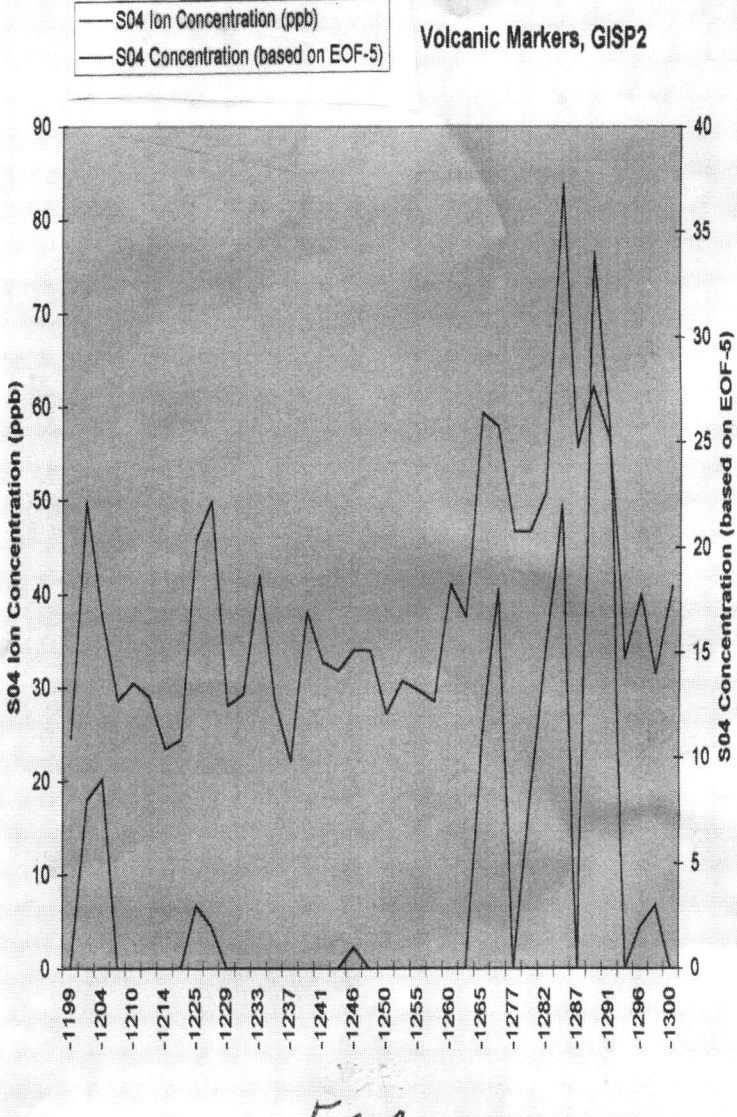

FIG. 2

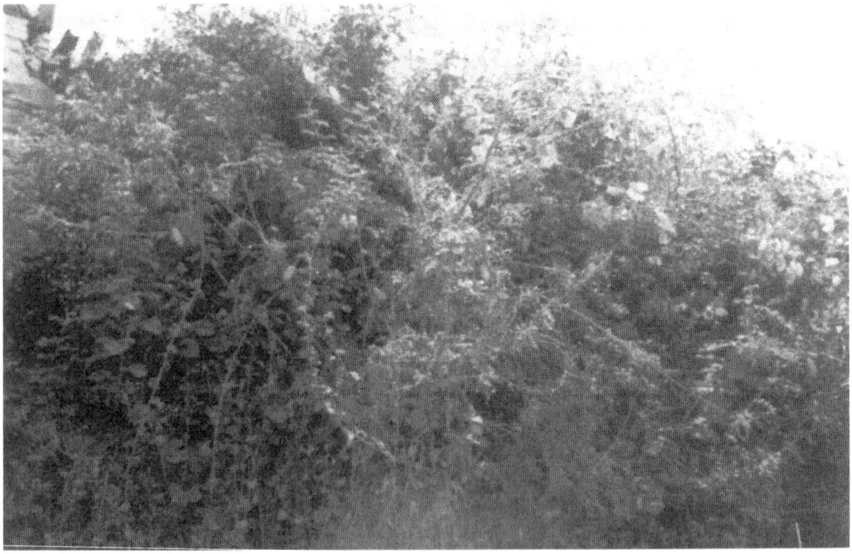

5

The Time Line of Events

"Mankind may supply us with facts, but the results, even if they agree with previous ones, must be the work of our mind".
—Benjamin Disraeli

The quest for the truth surrounding the events leading to the EXODUS, cannot be stated as plausible, without a showing of coinciding time lines of the cataclysms on Thera (Santorini Island), with the suspected date of the Exodus itself. And like all mysteries, there is always conflicting data.

Radiocarbon dating a trusted scientific tool, predicts the date of the initial eruption of Thera as occurring at 1628/7 B.C.[1]

The date of 1627/8 is also supported by corroborating data with the use of dendrochronology.

Gregory Zielinski, and Mark Germani were investigating a cataclysmic time of 1,623 B.C.. Their article entitled: "New Ice-Core Evidence Challenges the 1,620s BC age for the Santorini Explosion," Journal of Archaeological Science, Volume 25, Issue 3, Pages 279–289 (1998), brought into serious doubt that this date could be correct. They concluded that the glass contained in the volcanic dust was not the same as that found at Thera (Santorini). What they didn't do, however, is to comment on the fact that the data reveals only one large spike in the ice-core data for 1,623 B.C. This would have cast further doubt on this date, because every scientist and archaeologist now believes that there had to be a prior eruption before the blast that blew the island apart. In addition, a small prior spike to 1,623 B.C., would not have correlated with an eruption that covered Akrotiri with fifteen feet of pumice.

---

1. Some Egyptologist believe that radiocarbon dating does not apply to Egypt. The Stuarts (renowned Egyptologists) disparage the radiocarbon dating as inaccurate for Egyptian dating.

I have looked at the data (See Fig. 1) in a different way. These wonderful scientists were trying to prove, or disprove a cataclysm of Santorini at about 1,627 B.C. Instead, I sought to corrobate the data on the charts to coincide with the biblical text. The date I originally sought was circa. 1,450 B.C. I looked at the data as causing havoc throughout the whole Mediterranean Sea, including Egypt; keeping in mind the generally accepted date of the Exodus at 1,447 B.C.

To my amazement, when I was looking at the data from the ice-cores (Fig. 1), I discovered four closely grouped spikes at circa. 1,450 B.C. Each scale reading on the graph represents two years. The last spike was one and one-half as large as the first large spike. This fit the facts of the eruption/blast theory of the archaeologists.

The Greenland ice-core data suggests large eruptions prior to the main blast.

Thus, the ice-core data fits the Exodus date that is widely held, viz. circa 1,450 B.C.

When I first heard of the Thera explosion during my first visits to Santorini Island, I was informed that the best guess of its occurrence was about 1,750 B.C. Zielinski and Germani have also cast doubt on this date as well.

Later dating, as obtained from the internet at www.santorini.com places the time to be circa. 1,450–1,500 B.C. using archaeological pottery dating.

Dating of the eruption using archaeological pottery dating supports a date of about 1,450 to 1,500 B.C. The dating of pottery is pretty accurate, since the styles change with every generation.

But most important, the 1,450 B.C. date is corroborated by the biblical references.

As aforementioned, it appears more logical that the archaeological dating of Minoan pottery, which places the time frame for the eruptions and explosion of Thera at about 1450–1500 B.C., should be considered the true date in view of the ice-core data, and the biblical record. This is the same time frame as the scriptural dating of the Exodus of Moses (1447 B.C.), and the corroborating dates offered in the Encyclopedia Judaica, which suggest the EXODUS at about 1,450 B.C.

According to the Encylopedia Judaica, Book 6, Page 1043, 1973 Edition, the EXODUS in Kings 6:1 places the Exodus as no later than 1450–1430 B.C.E., (480 years before Solomon's temple) which is confirmed by Judges 11:26, which states that 300 years had elapsed from the entry of the Israelites into the land of Cannaan and the time of Jephthah, who judged during the second half of the 12th century B.C.

The whole region of the Mediterranean Sea had to be involved with the cataclysms, so it is only logical to combine the misfortunes of the Minoans with the events of the Hebrew Exodus from Egypt.

◆   ◆   ◆

Despite all of the corroborative evidence, however, the date of the Exodus at circa. 1,450 B.C. is nonetheless fraught with many difficulties. For one, this date would indicate that the pharaoh of the Exodus is Thutmoses II. But the biblical authorities in the Encylopedia Judaica do not accept the reign of Thutmoses II, as plausible, because he was a weak ruler. We are also faced with the fact that

Exodus 1:11 says that the Hebrew nation built the cities of Ramses and Pithom. This does not fit the reign of Thutmoses II.

And do I have to remind the reader, that Cecile B. DeMille in his movie, the Ten Commandments, seems to have had it right. The ancient historians Josephus and Philo by reason of their access to earlier biblical texts no longer available to us, had suggested the pharaoh was Ramses II. The building of the twin cities of Ramses and Pithom by the Hebrew nation, and the need for taskmasters, suggests the pharaoh is Ramses II. He was a stong ruler and a great builder. The city of Ramses carries his name.

Ramses II was the pharaoh with the 600 charioteers, as mentioned in the biblical text. The 600 charioteers is confirmed by recent excavations conducted in the Nile delta near the city of Tallen. These excavations have found the stables for six hundred chariots in the city of Ramses, which existed on what is now a dried tributary of the Nile.

As aforementioned, the biblical text has considered the possibility of Thutmoses II, but rejects this on the ground that he was a weak ruler. Weak rulers do not use taskmasters.

Authorities that I have read including the Stuarts, David Rohl, etc., each suggest pharaohs other than Ramses II. It is amazing to me, that there is so much variation in their research and the conclusions that they draw from it.

In addition, Bob Brier, Professor Emeritus from Long Island University, and of Discovery and Learning Channel fame, tells me that a colleague of his pointed to a Hebrew prophet that had mentioned that it was Ramses II as the Pharaoh of the Exodus. Unfortunately, he was unable to recall the exact text.

Bob Brier and I both believe Ramses II was the pharaoh of the Exodus. At least, we now have two researchers in agreement.

◆ ◆ ◆

The big problem, is the date of 1,450 B.C. This date is way too early for the reign of Ramses II, who supposedly ruled about 1,290 to 1,224 B.C. The 1,450 B.C. date does not coincide with the biblical text.

Steven McKenzie, in his article entitled: "Ramses II and the Bible", Rhodes College, obtained from the Wilbour Library, states that the date of 1,466 B.C. as derived from 1 Kings 6:1, is in error. The 480 years from Solomon's fourth year of reign was taken as 12 generations times 40 years. But he states that the average generation back then was 20 to 25 years, not forty years. Thus, he claims that this would make the time from 966 B.C., as 240 to 300 years, or between 1,266 and 1,206 B.C. This would then fit the reign of Ramses II. As with 1 Kings 6:1, scholars who accept the 13th century B.C. date for the Exodus, regard the 300 years in Judges 11:26 as artificial and secondary. The origin of the figure is unknown, but McKenzie believes that it may be an attempt to place the judges in consecutive order rather than treating them contemporaneously, which was often the case.

On the other hand, McKenzie says that the name Moses (Mosheh in the Hebrew) is an active participle meaning "drawing" not "drawn", so that in Exodus 2:10, the pharaoh's daughter would not have used the Hebrew term as "drawn" from the Nile. Rather, he says that Moses, is the same word part found in the names of Thutmosis, and Ahmose. The name means "God X is born". Thus,

Thutmoses means, Throth is born. Moses is therefore, a shortened form of such a name.

McKenzie also suggests that the biblical text was written down between 1,000 and 950 B.C., further casting doubt on the accuracy of the dates.

And every good mystery has a few corroborating clues as well as disparaging ones.

Leon Pomerance, in his article entitled: "The Final Collapse of Santorini (Thera), Studies in Mediterranean Archaeology, Vol. XXVI, Goteborg 1970, suggests that 1,400 B.C. is in doubt, because total devastation was recorded throughout the Mediterranean area about 1,200 B.C. He says, that if the magnitude of the depopulation that has so impressed all the authorities is correct, then the explosion of Thera appears to be the cause. The disappearance of complete towns suggests a massive tsunami that swept the towns out to sea circa. 1,200 B.C.

And in a later article, entitled "From Thera and the Aegean Word," Acta of Second International Scientific Congress, Aug. 1978, Leon Pomerance dismisses the pottery data as indicative of the cataclysm happening during the co-regency of Hatshepsut and Thutmose II, viz. 1,450 B.C.

Now, one may argue that with all the conflicting information, that we cannot trust the assertions made here? In every crime scene or mystery, detectives gather evidence. It is hard to trust evidence that is very old, because the eyewitnesses die, or their memories fade. Also, forensic evidence degrades with time. The various dates that are conflicting, are best guesses of learned men, who explore and excavate the sites of the ancient world. Even they will tell you that some of their determinations are best guesses that are based on other best guesses.

Biblical texts are trustworthy data. They have proven over time, that hidden places are just where they are claimed to be. Archaeologists usually find lost cities, after consulting biblical texts. Using data based upon these biblical texts, the archaeologists discern the coordinates of the lost cities, and more often than not, they prove accurate. This is true, even though some of the Exodus information had been written down hundreds of years later.

So, even though it is believed that scriptures, and the archaeological data are good sources of information, scientific data is definitely the best and most accurate source of information. That is the reason that I again turned to the data of the Greenland Ice-Cores for a clue.

I turned my attention to the Greenland ice-core data for the period of 1,300 to 1,200 B.C. (Please see Figure 2).

It is here that I found several large spikes in volcano SO_4 emissions about the time of 1,290 to 1,262 B.C. This time frame puts the eruptions squarely in the early reign of Ramses II. The most likely date would be 1,266 B.C., because it is after the battle of Kadesh reported to be 1,285 B.C., and appears to be the culmination of volcanic activity.

In the future, should some scientist verify that the glass of the ice-cores of either circa. 1,450 B.C. or 1,250 B.C. are those of Thera, it will be conclusive. No one can argue with the several spikes of the Greenland ice-core data.

The several spikes of volcanic activity in Fig. 2, fits the prevailing beliefs of what happened to the Minoan civilization at Akrotiri.

I believe that a better case is made for the time of 1,266 B.C. as the date of the Exodus.

I am comfortable in relying upon the scriptures, the research of Cecille B. DeMille, the ice-core data, and the two corroborating pieces (excavations near Tallen) suggesting Ramses II.

One last thought concerning David Rohl is in order, since he has created much discussion. It should be observed that most Egyptologists believe the present dynastic time line of the pharaohs is correct by reason that the dynastic time line interacts with the time lines of the Asyrians, Hittites, and Babylonians. Thus, it is truly a problem to assert that it is off. But if the time line was off two hundred years as Rohl suggests, than 1, 450 B.C. could be during the reign of Ramses II.

I reject this.

6

A Trip to Sinai

The plane engines droned a whining monotonous pitch, as we touched down in Saint Caterina, the Sinai. After passing through Egyptian customs, my daughter, Elena and I proceeded to the Monastery at the foot of the holy mountain where the Ten Commandments were supposedly received.

The monastery was constructed around 1,000 a.d.

The monk of the monastery had taken us to a mulberry bush located within its walls. The bush was fed by an under-ground spring. The monk suggested to the tourists that this was the burning bush. The bush was located at the base of the holy mountain, and should one like to know, it was claimed to be the only bush of its kind in the Sinai desert, or so he said. My daughter, Elena, and I yawned, took a picture, and moved on.

A few weeks later, the prints came back, and when we looked at the mulberry bush, a blue flame was situated inside. I cannot explain how this occurred, but it would be foolish to deny the power that such experiences bring to those of faith.

7

The Defining Moment

Many studies relate the Minoans demise to the cataclysms on Thera, but little concern or interest, it seems to me, is shown for the tsunami's effect on other lands, like Egypt. No one, has explored these events in detail, as they relate to the EXODUS. That is to say, it is my opinion that the emphasis of events of 1,450 B.C., or that of 1,266 B.C., have not been given more attention with respect to the EXODUS. I think that this is sad, because the EXODUS is the defining moment in history, when the Ten Commandments inextricably tied man to his God. If nothing more, it is one of the greatest mysteries of all time. I have also suggested that it is very short sighted to focus on the Minoans without examining the effect that the cataclysms of Thera had on the entire Mediterranean region.

I am not trying to be put a religious flavor to this story, but it seems to be obvious, that western civilization, Judaism, and Christianity would have evolved entirely differently, or not at all, had the events of the tsunami and the Exodus had not happened.

8

The Nature of Miracles

The pillar of flame that blocked the Egyptian advance towards the fleeing Hebrew nation is the most fascinating report of the entire story of the EXODUS. This sounds magical, and something only God would be able to achieve. It does not sound like any phenomena occurring on earth, and if it is to have credence in this story, then it must be addressed with a scientific approach.

I know that the explosion on Thera was the equivalent of many hydrogen bombs. It would not be too far fetched to imagine hot magma being hurled in a trajectory that would have spanned five hundred miles. Big Bertha, the huge cannon that the German's used in World War I, could fire a shell 75 miles towards Paris. Just up the scale a few hundred, or a few thousand, or a few million times. Put in perspective, it becomes logical to have the scenario that I have suggested. We know that hot magma reigned down on the palaces of the Minoans only 75 miles away. It is scientifically possible to have magma hurled hundreds of miles by an explosive force the equivalent of many hydrogen bombs.

The prior eruptions not only set in motion the Ten Plagues as previously discussed, but it also was the triggering mechanism for the explosion of the whole island of Thera.

These eruptions caused large cracks to form in the side of the mountain, and seawater poured through these vents. The water trickled down into the huge magma chamber below, and quickly turned to steam. The steam built up over time, and caused the whole island to explode. This is a common causation with sea volcanoes.

The Nature of Miracles 53

Some authorities place a fifty-year gap between the initial large eruption and the final cataclysmic explosion. Other sources say a generation past. This is not logical. The building of steam and pressure from the water leaking into the vents should be logically short in time. But the most cogent reason that the prior eruptions had to immediately precede the final explosion, is that it fits the biblical time line, and it appears to fit the ice-core data from Greenland.

The freeing of the Hebrew slaves in the biblical text suggests that the expulsion of the Hebrew nation immediately followed the Ten Plagues.

Would any pharaoh have waited a generation, or fifty years to ponder the question?

The final cataclysm is suggested as being shortly after the prior eruptions, by the ice-core spikes.

The guesses made by these archaeologists did not study the Greenland ice-core data.

◆ ◆ ◆

One must also ponder the economic destruction that the cataclysms had on the Mediterranean region.

As the Ten Plagues ravaged the Egyptians, Pharaoh grew weary of his Hebrew slaves. They were a large nation of mouths to feed, in an economy that had to have increasing shortages of food. It would be prudent to pause here, to consider that the initial Thera blast would also have had an immediate and short-range effect of cooling the earth, and the contamination of the land. The loss of food production would be obvious. The trade throughout the Mediterranean was severely effected as well.

Zielinski and Germani suggest that sulfurous emissions in the atmosphere are dissipated within a few years, yet high sulfurous content is evident throughout the thirteenth century B.C., as evidenced in Fig. 2.

Coupling this fact with the plagues and disease ravaging the twin cities of RAM-PI, one can accept the idea that the time had come for Ramses to send the Hebrew nation away for economic reasons as well as religious reasons.

So pharaoh may have decided that having slaves was no longer such an advantage, or maybe he feared the Hebrew God. In any event, he cast the Hebrew nation out of Goshen.

Having cast the Hebrews from his kingdom, pharaoh may have now realized that this had been a bad decision. He may have been losing control of his own people. Whispers and rumors could have flashed through the court. The highly superstitious Egyptian populace may have started to believe that the Hebrew God was a more powerful god, than the pharaoh.

Had Ramses succumbed to the Jewish God of the Hebrews? Was he weak? Was he a lesser god?

Ramses was now faced with a terrible decision. His people may have lost faith in his power to rule. He may have had to act quickly to counter this threat to his authority.

In any event, he decided to punish the Hebrew nation.

Ramses II now made ready his six hundred charioteers, in order to seek out, and destroy the Hebrew nation. Meanwhile, the pressure cooker of a mountain called Thera Island, was ready to explode. An explode it did. An explosion calculated to be three and one half to as much as fourteen times greater than the blast that pulverized Krakatoa in the Sea of Java, at the end of the nineteenth century.

The Nature of Miracles 55

The explosion was of monumental proportions. Hot magma was hurled at supersonic speed from the magma chamber, as the walls of the mountain turned to dust. The surrounding Aegean Sea was shocked and displaced, and produced a MEGA-TSUNAMI of enormous proportions. Two hundred feet of wave spread out in all directions from the blast, reaching speeds approaching 200 miles per hour. The wave was only five hundred miles in a straight line from the Nile delta and the Sea of Reeds.

◆ ◆ ◆

The racing chariots of pharaoh approached the Hebrew nation as they were preparing to cross the Sea of Reeds that lay contiguous to the Goshen area. As the charioteers were in sight of their prey, the Mega-Tsunami, was rolling towards the Nile delta shore. The water would eventually begin to recede, and the Hebrews would start a hasty crossing through the draining swamp towards higher ground.

The hot sheets of molten magma started to descend from the skies in front of the Egyptian warriors, and gave the large contingent of Hebrews time to move towards safety. This "pillar of flame" blocked the Egyptian advance for some time, and they had to wait. The sheets of flame arrived before the Mega-Tsunami rolled to shore, by reason of their higher velocity.

The Egyptians saw the Hebrew nation crossing the Sea of Reeds in great haste, but they were powerless to pursue.

As the aerial events started to subside, the Hebrews had reached their perch on the far side of the Sea of Reeds. The unknowing Egyptians now thought it was their turn to race across the seabed. They were totally unprepared for what happened next. They did not know about tsunamis. They did not realize the danger that awaited them as they raced towards the drained swamp.

Inexorably, and swiftly, the two hundred foot wall of water engulfed them. The wave having gained height and momentum by the water that had rushed out to greet it, now ominously had moved on shore.

The charioteers were gone within minutes. Their chariots were hurled into the sea, as the wave passed over them. Eyewitnesses not understanding what they had observed, probably could not fathom a wall of water to their right and left.

And indeed, it is not hard to argue, that a divine presence was at work here. Just consider that the precise timing of the event is incredible. It can be argued with much cogency, that the God of the Hebrew nation had used natural forces to free the "chosen ones". He had triggered the events to provide the result at the time it was needed, and such is the nature of miracles.

Please understand, that although there is good reason to attribute this miracle to God, one can rest the event on the shoulders of science, if one so chooses.

Natural science is clearly at work here.

This story allows space to comfortably occupy a position in both science and/or religion. I for one believe that God and science are synonymous. As a world traveler I believe in the power of science and God. I have seen the beauty of this planet. And I have also seen the tremendous forces at work about the earth. Forces of great magnitude that shaped the events of the EXODUS and that of the "chosen" messengers of the Ten Commandments,…the Hebrew nation.

9

Hatshepsut Leads the Way

My trip to Egypt had taken me to the wonderful temple in the Valley of the Kings built by Hatshepsut, the queen pharaoh who had grown up as an astute little girl in the court of Tutmoses II. Hatshepsut loved the intrigues of the royal court, and was very clever in obtaining the throne for herself, when Thutmoses II suddenly died. The only heir apparent to the throne was a boy of nine, Thutmoses III. It was obvious that he could not rule, so Hatshepsut suggested that as an interim measure, she would handle the affairs of the Egyptian kingdom as a vizier. Later, she announced that she was pharaoh.

Many years later, when the boy had reached manhood, Hatshepsut shared the throne with him. Her rule was marked with peace and prosperity. Thutmoses III loved military campaigns, and conducted several incursions into foreign lands.

The transition to the throne was easy for Hatshepsut, since she was already doing the work of a pharaoh as vizier. However, she must have experienced much prejudice. Like the prejudices of today, woman then, were not considered worthy of such a high post.

Hatshepsut knew that she had two big obstacles to overcome: (1) the fact that never before had there been a woman pharaoh, and (2) that she was not in the line of succession to the throne. This did not stop this lady. Carefully, she used propaganda to persuade her detractors.

Hatshepsut carved on the steles of her temple in the Valley of the Kings, a story wherein she makes sacrifice to the head God Isis and her falcon-headed son Horus, and they grant her the throne of Egypt, both the upper and lower regions.

Now, would any one doubt the word of the God Isis? Hardly not, and so was born a new pharaoh.

So you may ask, what relevance this has with our story of Ramses II? I thought he may have used this idea to counter the voices criticizing him as a weaker god than the Hebrew God. This technique, however, became a teaching tool for other pharaohs, including Ramses II. Yes! He may have used the same technique to quell the rising voices of his detractors after the EXODUS, but it is not proof that he was pharaoh of the Exodus. (I refer you to one of the figures in this book, showing Ramses II making an offering to the Goddess Isis and her falcon-headed son Horus).

10

A Papyrus Shop in Cairo

The art of making paper had its origins with papyrus paper, whose process dates back some five thousand years ago. The modern word: "paper" derives from the Egyptian word: "papyrus". The art of making papyrus paper was lost in antiquity until recently, when an Egyptian professor figured out the secret of its manufacture.

Papyrus paper is made from the papyrus plant that grows abundantly along the Nile. Its long stem provides a graceful look to the plant.

Papyrus, the plant, is highly considered by the Egyptians. This plant is revered as a thing of beauty, and is featured on many of their decorations.

The long stem is stiff and inflexible. Slicing the stem into slivers, it is impossible to weave the strips into an interlocking matrix. Yet, that is how papyrus was made in ancient times. The strips were woven into a sheet of paper.

So, how did the Egyptians do it?

The professor soaked the strips of papyrus in water for several days. During that time, the sugars in the cells of the plant dissolved and leached out. This made the strips supple and flexible. After weaving the strips to form a sheet, the water was pressed out of the papyrus cells, and the new sheet of paper was left in the sun to dry.

◆ ◆ ◆

Having essentially completed my trip to Egypt, it was time to buy gifts to bring home to my friends and family. Celia, my green-eyed lady, and I, hopped into a cab outside our Cairo hotel.

After negotiating a price with the driver for an all day trip about the city, we headed to a gift shop and purchased a lovely chess set of ivory, for her brother Milton. In those days, ivory could be purchased freely, and I suspect that one could still find some shops that sell it. I would not recommend that one do this, however, because such items are now confiscated by customs.

From the gift shop, we wandered down the street to a Papyrus Shop. The shop was filled with painted scrolls of Egyptian hieroglyphics. I was told that the workmen painting the hieroglyphics obtained the various texts from museum brochures featuring interesting statements carved upon the steles. I decided to purchase a few scrolls. One in particular was intriguing for it had Ramses II making an offering to the gods Isis and her falcon-headed son. In return, Horus, her falcon-headed son, and Isis were granting Ramses II the throne of Egypt; both the throne to upper and lower Egypt, as exemplified by the two crowns of upper and lower Egypt they wore on their heads.

This was odd, because Ramses II was already pharaoh, and he was one of the greatest kings. He did not need to do this.

Originally, it had dawned upon me, that after the EXODUS, people were questioning his authority as pharaoh. Therefore, it appeared that Ramses II had used the same technique that Hatshepsut had used to convince the people that he had godly authority to rule.

I thought this was significant, because it was one of the only clues that indicate the EXODUS took place in the reign of Ramses II. This scroll, however, did not corroborate that it was Ramses II as the Exodus pharaoh. The fact was, as Bob Brier clearly corrected me, all the pharaohs did this. And not only did they do this, they did this all the time.

11

Disaster

The word disaster comes from the Greek word "astron" meaning star, and disaster literally translates as not in the stars. People in ancient times believed that our destiny was in the stars, and the many devotees of horoscopes are their descendents.

The events that befell the Minoans, and Egypt, were truly disasters. The eruption and explosion on Thera Island was an enormous disaster by any present measurable standards to which it can be compared.

The description of how the Hebrew nation left Egypt is not speculative. Consider this! We now know from recent reports and television commentary that the recent Sumatra tsunami, which was only twenty feet high, caused enormous damage. What would a two hundred foot tsunami do?

Also consider this, the first eruptions were greater blasts than most eruptions of modern times. The dusts would have lingered in the atmosphere for many years, blocking the sunlight, and cooling the earth. The explosion would have further added considerably to the airborne particulate.

The people at that time would have experienced a colder climate, and food production would have suffered.

The Hebrew nation was cast out of Egypt into the Sinai, a normally blistering desert. Perhaps some good came of the cataclysms, because the desert may have become a more comfortable place with the cooling of the earth.

It is like the old adage: "It is an ill wind, that does not blow some good."

The prevailing view of most people who experience disasters of this kind, is that any good they do is not worth it.

Yet, ponder this: the natural tectonic movement of the earth, is a continuous process of destruction and renewal. When volcanoes erupt, they distribute materials that make the land more fertile. Every time you eat an Idaho potato, consider the fact that it tastes so good because it has been grown in volcanic soil.

Ladies, when you wear your engagement ring with its sparkling diamond, think of the pressures and temperatures in the tectonic plates that formed the lovely diamond.

12

The Ten Commandments

The world misinterprets the statement that the "Jews are the chosen people". God has never intended to play favorites with mankind. The Hebrew nation is not regarded any differently than any one else in God's eyes. The Hebrew nation is only given privilege as messengers of God. What does this mean? As messengers, they were chosen to receive the Ten Commandments for mankind.

Consider this: would not the world be a much better place, if all the people acted kindly towards one another? Acts of kindness are truly man's only hope.

All the violence, hatred, and unkind acts detract from our humanity, and diminish all mankind.

The Ten Commandments are great rules for a good life.

In sending the Hebrew nation into the Sinai before the great holy mountain, was it God or man who fashioned the Ten Commandments?

Do these words not speak of divine understanding? Even to those who are not religious, the words of the Ten Commandments have sacred meaning. Western civilization, its laws, and its framework for society are based on the Ten Commandments.

This was a defining moment in history!

13
A Divine Plan?

The Hebrew Joseph, went down into Egypt as a slave, so it is written in the biblical text. He rose to become the vizier of Pharaoh, and the Hebrew nation flourished. But succeeding pharaohs decided to enslave the Hebrews. The Hebrew nation endured under this tyranny for four hundred and thirteen years.

Why, if there is a God of Israel, did he not act sooner? Why did he just bring the plagues sooner? What was the divine plan?

For those of you who want a scientific explanation, please consider this: it took four hundred years for the magma in the Thera mountain to gather in the magma chamber in sufficient quantity to produce eruptions of sufficient magnitude that would block out the sun for three days and create tsunamis that rescued the Hebrew nation at the Sea of Reeds.

To the scientist, some volcanoes blow quickly, and some hang around dormant for hundreds and thousands of years. It is all a matter of plate tectonics.

Eruptions take time. Mount Saint Helens erupted after many years of subduction of the tectonic plate below the western coast of the United States. It was twenty years before the magma built sufficiently to cause the mountain to erupt again.

Time was needed for magma to build in the magma chamber at Thera. God must obey his own laws of physics and natural phenomena.

Earth, science, and God work on a grand scale. As humans, we are only around for a blink of celestial time. We cannot fathom the enormity of space, the eons of time needed to fashion a planet, or the divine plan. We are just transient observers in a world that ticks on celestial time. We just burn out too fast. We never see the whole picture.

◆   ◆   ◆

Many years ago, I had a dog that wished to go outside. I could not take him for a walk, because it was raining a ton. He signaled that he adamantly wanted to go out, by slamming his front paw upon the floor, near the front door. I shook my head. He again slammed his paw on the floor. I realized he could not understand that there was rain outside. After all, he was behind the door. I understood, because I had the whole picture. I saw beyond the door. All of a sudden, I had an epiphany. It occurred to me, that we stand in our relationship to God, like my puppy waiting in front of the door. We just do not see the whole picture.

God works on celestial time, and in long sweeping arcs. It is only years later that I often come to understand the events of 10 or 15 years earlier.

14

Mega Tsunamis and Other Cataclysmic Events Yet to Come

As an American, I often forget, that the United States is in potential danger of two potentially cataclysmic events. There is a enormous magma chamber below Yellowstone National Park. The magma chamber extends across the whole park, and is slowly filling, as witnessed by the overflow of its lake over the last 75 years. Should there ever be an explosion or eruption in this area, it would wipe out a major portion of the United States.

In the Canary Islands there is an island called: La Palma. It is an unstable volcanic mountain, whose soil has already shifted towards the sea on its western boundary. It is estimated by scientists, that should this island have a volcanic event, the earth could slide into the Atlantic ocean, creating a Mega-Tsunami that would roll towards the east coast of the United States at a speed of six hundred miles and hour. The wave could be as high as two hundred feet or more. Can any one imagine a wall of water that big hitting Manhattan? Our government needs to work out some details with Spain on how to stabilize the earth on this island. It would make sense to spend the money to fix the problem, before the problem becomes unfixable, and we have to spend additional monies to repair and reconstruct the damage.

Our government, like other governments always seems powerless to attack a problem until that problem is right on the door step. We, however, should not be critical of this, because we as individuals are not usually any better.

15

A Walk Along the Country Road

The wandering of the Hebrew nation in Sinai may be the result of many factors, some of which I already mentioned. With the destruction of the golden trade route between Alexandria, Iraklion, and Ephesis, the economy of the whole region was destroyed. The winter-like climate may have assisted a prolonged visitation in the dessert. The harshness of the terrain was surely a problem.

Perhaps this was a time for the Hebrew nation to find its identity. After being slaves for four hundred years, the unshackled minds of the people may have needed time to breath the fresh air of freedom.

Prior to receiving the Ten Commandments at the holy mountain, the Hebrew nation threw a poorly planned party, wherein they defamed themselves before the Lord.

Our present day teenagers throw some pretty bad parties. What it all seems to indicate, is that societies and people need to assess their responsibilities towards themselves, each other, and their neighbors.

The Ten Commandments were, and still are, good guideposts along the roadway towards a responsible and meaningful life.

As a young man, I used to take my daughter of seven or eight for walks along the country road to the malt shop. Of all the gifts and kindnesses that I have since bestowed upon her through the years, she always tells me that those were the happiest moments in her life.

So what does this all mean?

I believe that we are all seeking to find our way, like the wandering Hebrew nation. We have a choice to act as responsible human beings, to love our neighbors, and to do acts of kindness. Otherwise, we shall lose our way in a desert of unfulfilled promises.

The encyclopedia Judaica suggests many different routes to the land of Caanan. The text in Volume 6, Page 1043–1050 suggests different sites for the holy mountain.

The travels through Sinai shall be the inspiration of my next book.

16
Reprise

I have suggested that science and God work together, because God made the science and physics, which control the destiny of men.

I desire for scientists, Rabbis, priests and clergymen to agree with this thought.

It is explained that there has been logic, science and economic reasons for the basis of events that fashioned the story of the EXODUS. I am not alone in these thoughts. Many archaeologists agree with many of the thoughts I have put together in this book. I hope that the data and thoughts that I have presented will be acceptable to the general public, for I believe that I am right.

I have stated that humanity is diminished by murder and violence. The Ten Commandments are key to our survival. It is hoped that the reader shall look upon the Ten Commandments in a new light. It is hoped that terrorists, and people of violence will realize that their actions are detrimental to all mankind.

There is a place in our world for men of peace. Martin Luther King, Jr., and Mahatma Ghandi were truly instrumental in bringing about change through peaceful resistance. Peaceful resistance trumps violence every time. Even Mahmoud Abas, the newly elected leader of the Palestinians, has recently stated that the violence that Hamas has wrought on Israel has only hurt the Palestinian people.

Let us learn from the past, that it is important to conduct our lives with acts of kindness, so that we may lead useful lives and enrich and ennoble society.

A Final Word From the Author

Writing this book has left me with a feeling of the awesome power of nature, and because I am a religious man, an appreciation of the awesome power of God.

What strikes me as very unique is the final punishment that God enacted upon the Egyptian people. It was not the taking of many lives. It was much more than that.

Let me explain.

The Egyptian nation went into serious decline after the Exodus. One can blame their failure to survive as a nation, to their inability to make iron weapons; for Egypt, had no iron deposits. Their copper weapons were no match against the iron weapons of their enemies.

However, there is something more basic here; something that speaks of true punishment on a Godly scale. What I am referring to is the fact that the entire nation of Egyptians was erased. Their language was erased. Nothing remains of them, but their writings and monuments.

The Egyptians of today, are not the true Egyptians of Ramses' time. The Egyptians of today are Arabs, who think of themselves as Egyptians. The Arabs in Egypt are very proud of their heritage, and I do not mean to take this away from them.

But is it truly their heritage, or identity?

I do not know. The original Egyptians clearly had to assimilate with other tribes. The old Egyptian nation was slowly swallowed up in time. Enemies and external forces destroyed their civilization, and they are gone forever.

This truly speaks of Godly punishment.

Even the Romans who destroyed the second temple of Israel in 70 A.D. did not suffer such a fate. It is true that they too are gone forever, but Latin, their language survives.

Therefore, I believe that the Egyptians were severely punished for enslaving the Hebrew nation far beyond any other nation who wrought evil against them.

Index

A

Aaron, 19
Abbas, Mahmoud, 82
Ahmose, 42
Akrotiri, lost city of, 4–7
   abandonment of, by Minoans, 7
   discovery of, 4–5
Alexandria, 7, 78
astron, 66

B

Ba'al-ze'phon, 26, 28–29
bloom, algal, 9, 17, 20
Brier, Bob, 41–42, 63

C

Crete, 6

D

DeMille, Cecil B., xiii, 41, 45
disasters, 66–67

E

Egypt. *See also* pharaoh of Egypt
   effect of Thera explosion on, 53–54, 66
   escape of Hebrews from, xii, 55–56
Ephesis, 7, 78
eruption, volcanic
   at Herculaneum, 7
   of Mount St. Helens, 17, 23
   at Pompei, 7
   at Santorini (Thera), 7–9, 19–25, 38
Exodus, date of, xii, 40, 44

F

frescoes. *See* Minoans

G

Germani, Mark, 38, 54
Ghandi, Mahatma, 82
Golden Trade Triangle, 7, 78

Goshen, town of, 12, 18, 20–21, 24–25, 28, 54–55

H

hail, 22
Hatshepsut, 43, 58
Hebrew nation, 70
    captivity of, 19–25, 53–54, 72
    escape from Egypt, xii
    expulsion and pursuit of, by pharaoh, 25–29, 54
Herculaneum, 7

I

ice cores, Greenland, xi, xiii, 8, 38–39, 44, 53
    glass in, xiv, 38, 44
Indian Ocean, xiv
inversions, atmospheric, 22
Iraklion, port of, 6, 7, 13

J

Joseph, 72
Josephus, xiii, 41

K

Kadesh, battle of, 44
Kaikos, island of, 27

King, Martin Luther, Jr., 82
Krakatoa island, explosion of, 8, 54

L

La Palma, unstable volcanic island of, 76
Lee, Jeffrey A., 16
lightning, 22
locusts, 22

M

Marinatos, Spirodin, 4–7
McKenzie, Steven, 42
Minoans, 50
    frescoes of, 4–5
    palaces of Minos, 6
    pottery of, 39–40
Moses, 19–25, 41–42
Mount St. Helens, eruption of, 17, 23, 72

N

Nile delta, 8–9, 12

P

papyrus paper, 62
Parting of the Sea, xii, 12–13, 16, 27–29, 55–56

peace, 82
pharaoh of Egypt, xii–xiii, 12, 40–43, 58, 63. *See also individual pharaohs*
   and captivity of Hebrews, 19–25
   expulsion and pursuit of Hebrews by, 25–29
Philo, xiii, 41
Pi-ha-Hi'roth, 26
Pillar of Fire, 28, 52, 55
Pithom, city of, xiii, 8, 17, 18, 23, 41
plague, 24–25
Pomerance, Leon, 43
Pompei, 7
pottery, Minoan, 39–40, 43
pyroclastic flows, 7

R

radiocarbon dating, 38
Ram-Pi. *See* Pithom, city of; Ramses, city of
Ramses, city of, xiii, 8, 17, 18, 23, 41
Ramses II, xiii, 41–42, 44–45, 58–59, 63
red tide (algal bloom), 9, 17, 20
Rohl, David, 45

S

Santorini island (Thera), xi, xiii–xiv, 2, 4, 12, 38, 50
   explosion of, 7–9, 52–53, 54, 66, 72
science and faith, 56, 72, 82
Sea of Reeds, xii, 12–13, 27, 55, 72
   "Yam Suph," 28
Sethi, xiii
Sinai, 48, 70, 78–79

T

Tallen, city of, 41, 45
Ten Commandments, xi, 48, 50, 70, 78, 82
Ten Commandments, The (Cecil B. DeMille), xiii, 41
Ten Plagues, 16, 19–25, 52–53
Thera, island of. *See* Santorini island
Thutmoses II, 40–43, 58
Thutmoses III, 58
tsunamis, 66
   impending, 76
   at Iraklion, 6
   Parting of the Sea as, 16–17, 27–29, 55–56

V

Valley of the Kings, 58
Vesuvius, 7

W

Wilbour Library (Brooklyn Museum), xi, xiii

Y

Yam Suph, 28. *See also* Sea of Reeds
Yellowstone National Park, magma chamber beneath, 76

Z

Zielinski, Gregory, 38, 54

978-0-595-34797-1
0-595-34797-5